Tasting Coffee

Coffee Cupping Techniques

to Unleash the Bean!

By

Jessica Simms

Tasting Coffee: Coffee Cupping Techniques to Unleash the Bean!

Warning and Disclaimer

Every effort has been made to make this book as accurate as possible. However, no warranty or fitness is implied. The information provided is on an "as-is" basis. The author and the publisher shall have no liability or responsibility to any person or entity with respect to any loss or damages that arise from the information in this book.

Publisher Contact

Skinny Bottle Publishing

books@skinnybottle.com

SKINNY BOTTLE

The Idea Behind Coffee Tasting

There is both an art and a science to tasting coffee. The overall flavor profile of coffee is assertive and distinctive; if you've never tried to identify the specific notes, you may just think that every cup you drink simply tastes like coffee, especially if you typically add milk and sugar to your beverages. The truth is, though, that there are a lot of subtle variations and flavor differences between different cultivars and varieties, as well as between coffees that have been grown, processed, or roasted differently. Being able to identify these differences can open up a whole new world of coffee for you to enjoy.

When people talk about the flavor notes of coffee, this doesn't mean that the coffees themselves have been flavored. Rather, this is referring to the other flavors that are developed within the bean and add complexity to the overall flavor profile. Picking these notes out from each other can be tricky, especially for the novice taster, requiring both practice and attention to identify. The good news is you don't need to be a barista to taste these subtle notes. A well-trained palate can be developed over time, even if you have no professional experience in coffee.

The idea behind a coffee tasting is to isolate the specific characteristics of a single variety. While you can do a tasting with blends, you'll get more value out of tasting single-origin coffees, since this will allow you to more clearly identify the specific taste characteristics in that bean. It's important to maintain uniformity throughout and across the samples, as well, to avoid adding any extra flavor variations into the mix, like those caused by different roast levels, grind levels, and brew methods.

Even between exceptional coffees, not all of them will taste the same. The goal with coffee is not to produce beans of identical quality but to bring out the maximum potential of each bean—in other words, having it be the best version of itself. Some coffees will have more sweetness, and some more acidity; some will be velvety in the texture, while others will be thinner in your mouth. Part of the purpose of a tasting is to identify which qualities of coffee are most appealing to you and finding the beans that exhibit all of those characteristics.

Tasting coffee first means understanding the flavors it contains and how to identify them yourself. Both sides of this are explored in the chapters that follow in this book. Just like with wine, there is a community and tradition built around tasting coffee, and industry professionals have designed flavor wheels that identify some of the key flavor notes and other attributes found in many coffees. Studying and understanding these will be a great benefit in setting up your own tasting, but will be useless if you haven't developed your palate to be able to detect subtleties of flavor. Knowledge and skill must be built up together for a truly successful tasting.

Chapter 1: Supplies for Home Tasting

For the most part, the supplies you need for setting up a coffee tasting at home are the same ones you'll use for general brewing, but there are some specialized pieces of equipment that will be helpful to have on hand. If you want to get the professional tasters' version of this equipment, you can buy it online from the Specialty Coffee Association of America (SCAA, for short), but you can also use things that you have around your own home or buy less expensive versions of the same basic tools from your local kitchen supply or department store.

The idea behind a coffee tasting is to get as true a sense as possible of what notes and flavor characteristics the bean exhibits. This means you'll want to limit as many variables as possible that could change the consistency of your brew or alter the flavor of the bean. It's imperative that you grind the beans at home, immediately before brewing, to avoid the loss of volatile compounds that contribute to the coffee's flavor and aroma. Similarly, you'll want to weigh the beans and use a specific quantity of water, even if you're typically in the habit of eyeballing these amounts, so you can be sure differences in flavor are due to differences in the bean and not variations in the brewing method.

Because of this, the kinds of supplies you'll need to actually purchase before setting up your own home coffee tasting will vary greatly depending on how sophisticated your current brewing set-up is. If you already have a burr grinder and a gram scale, for example, your purchases will be minimal; if you typically use pre-ground coffee, on the other hand, you'll need to spend a bit of extra money to get the right equipment before attempting a tasting.

The sections that follow in this chapter will walk you through every piece of equipment required for a tasting, why you need it, and what kind you should buy. Coffee tasting is a time-sensitive process. The taste and aroma of coffee can change significantly as it brews and then cools. Achieving perfect consistency in all the samples means being able to grind, brew, and taste all of your samples on the same basic schedule. Because of this, you'll probably find it best to not only purchase all of your supplies before starting, but also to assemble them in one place for easy access before you pour your first beans into the grinder.

Cups

There are two sets of cups that you'll need for setting up your own home cupping lab: the containers for holding the portioned-out beans in preparation for brewing, and the glasses you'll be brewing into. The containers that you portion the beans into don't have to follow any specific guidelines, so long as they'll hold enough beans for a single brew. Small bowls, Tupperware containers, or disposable plastic or paper cups will function nicely for your purposes. You could even use extra coffee filters or cupcake wrappers in a pinch.

The brewing cups need to follow slightly more stringent guidelines. They should have a capacity of around 5-7 ounces, and should be approximately the same size. You should also pick a cup made of a material with a relatively good heat retention. Ceramic and glass are ideal. Rocks glasses (like those used for many mixed drinks) tend to be a good option, but you can also use dishes or bowls, provided they have the right volume. Whatever kind of vessel you brew in, you should make sure that it has a relatively wide mouth, at least wide enough for two spoons at once so that you can properly skim the grinds off of the top during the process.

How many bean containers and brewing glasses you need will depend on how many samples you want to test at one time. If you're tasting with a group of four or more, you will likely want to have two cups for each type of coffee you're testing so that everyone will get the same opportunity to taste and smell the brewed beverage. Many professional tasters will brew three versions of each sample as a matter, of course, to account for potential inconsistencies in the roast or bean and make sure they're getting a thorough profile of the coffee in question. As a home taster, you can choose whether or not you want to follow this same pattern; it may be a factor of how many cups you have available to use.

Spoons

Like with the cups, professional tasters use specialized spoons for sampling. These are shallower and wider than the average spoon from your silverware drawer and are also typically silver-plated. This is more than simply aesthetics; spoons made of steel, plastic, or other materials can subtly alter the taste of the coffee that you're sampling.

For home tasting, you don't necessarily need to worry about the material that's been used in making your spoon, although metal is generally better than plastic. The main thing you should pay attention to is the size and shape of the spoon. You want something that's shallower and wider than the typical spoon you'd use to eat your cereal in the morning. If you can find soup spoons, these will work better than standard spoons for tasting purposes.

You won't need quite as many spoons as you do cups for your tasting because you won't need a designated spoon for each sample, provided you keep a cup of clean water on the tasting table to rinse the spoon between coffees. A set of four total spoons should be sufficient, regardless of how many coffees you're tasting.

Scale

Different coffee beans will have different densities depending on their growing conditions and roast level. Because of this, weight is a much more accurate way to measure coffee than volume, and since accuracy and consistency are paramount in coffee tasting, you'll need to have a scale to do it effectively.

A digital scale with gram measurements is going to be your best bet. Dial scales simply will not give you the degree of accuracy and precision you'll want for a truly successful tasting. Look for one that can measure with a precision of at least .1 grams (.01 grams is even better). If you don't already have one, you can buy a fairly reliable and effective one for around $30 from most kitchen supply and department stores.

Grinder

Likely the most expensive piece of equipment you'll need to buy if you don't have one already is a quality burr grinder. Blade coffee grinders are inexpensive, but they can't give you the grind consistency you need either between or within batches to really get a sense of the different flavors. This is because the fineness of the grind in a blade grinder is based on how long it runs, leading to a large variation between the different pieces that result, and making it much harder to get the grind to the same level every time. With a burr grinder, the coffee beans crushed between metal plates, with the distance between them determining the grind size, allowing for far more control.

There are different styles of burr grinders. Generally speaking, the more expensive the model, the more fine-tuning it allows on the part of the brewer. Because you'll be using an immersion method to brew for a tasting, you don't need to worry about getting a high-end espresso grinder. You can find a reliable burr grinder for around $100 to $200. While this might seem like a hefty investment, it will also improve the quality of your coffee drinking experience, regardless of your brewing method.

Kettle and water

You will need to have some way to heat your water for your brew. It's not recommended to heat up your water in the microwave or in a saucepan on the stovetop; this can give it a flat taste that affects the flavor of the cup. Either an electric or a stovetop kettle should suit your needs nicely. While gooseneck kettles can be helpful in controlling the amount of water that comes out at any given time, they're not strictly necessary for coffee tasting the way they are for manual brewing methods like pour over and Chemex. More important than the way the water pours is that you are able to pour the same amount consistently in each tasting cup.

When it comes to what kind of water you use, this will likely be a factor of the area where you live. If the water that comes out of your tap has a relatively low mineral content, you should have no problem using it to brew your tasting samples. If the water is especially hard, contains high amounts of chemicals like chlorine, or if there is a lime scale problem in your region, you may want to consider bottled options. Most brewers recommend avoiding distilled water, as this can make your coffee taste flat, in a similar way to heating the water in a microwave. Whether you use filtered water, natural spring water, or reverse osmosis water is up to you. Again, the main thing that's important is consistency across tastings.

Coffee

Obviously, the most important aspect of any coffee tasting is the coffee itself. You'll want to have a range of coffees to compare to each other. You should use at least three different varieties to give you an adequate range of flavors. Each tasting portion will use around 12 grams of coffee. A quarter pound of each variety you're tasting should be more than enough for two tasting portions and a bit left over in case you make a mistake along the way.

You can use any coffee that you want to for a coffee tasting, but you should consider the roast level before you buy. Dark roasts will obscure some of the original flavors of the bean; a light or medium roast will reveal more of the true nature of the coffee. If the surface of the coffee bean is shiny, it's probably roasted too dark to use in this context. When you're first starting out, you'll find it more valuable to choose beans with a wide range

9

of flavor profiles. It will be easier to taste the differences between an Ethiopia and a Sumatra, for example, than to pick out a Guatemala from a Costa Rica. As you gain more experience, you can narrow your selections, tasting coffees grow in more closely related regions—or even different processing methods or farms within the same region—to note the subtle changes.

Tasting journal

When professional coffee tasters cup their beans, they have forms that they fill out, with designated spaces to grade and evaluate various aspects of the drinking experience. You certainly don't need to go to this extreme with your home tastings, but keeping a journal or a book of notes is likely to be beneficial. By recording what you taste in various coffees when you cup them, you can hone in on which beans produce flavors that you like. This will help you establish a frame of reference for your future tastings, honing and developing your palate.

Chapter 2: The Taster's Vocabulary

It's one thing to be able to taste the different notes and textures that a certain bean produces, but this won't be very helpful if you don't have the language to express it. If you have some experience with wine tasting, many of these terms will be familiar to you, but coffee does have its own set of terminology and common flavor characteristics that even experienced sommeliers will have to learn.

When it comes to the flavor notes themselves, it's more about being able to pick out specific tastes than it is learning words. Where a lot of the confusion over coffee tasting comes into play is with the overarching flavor descriptors and the terms that describe various aspects of the mouthfeel or texture. The sections that follow in this chapter will give you a brief introduction to these categorical terms, what the specific designations mean, and the impact they have on the flavor of your final cup.

Taste versus aromatics

The flavor of a coffee is a combination of two distinct categories of compounds: aromatics and tastes. Aromatic compounds are extremely volatile. They begin to dissipate into the atmosphere as soon as you grind the coffee, and once they've evaporated into the atmosphere they cannot be recovered. This means they're also readily extracted by hot water and are often the first things to dissolve into the cup of coffee. In terms of the overall weight of the coffee bean, they comprise only a negligible amount, but they have a huge impact on your perception of the coffee's taste. The continued evaporation of aromatic compounds over time is one of the reasons that coffee changes flavor so dramatically as it cools, and is also why it's generally best to enjoy your coffee immediately after preparation.

Taste compounds, on the other hand, extract more slowly. These come from water-soluble, non-volatile compounds like caffeine, carbohydrates, and trigonelline. They do not dissipate after the coffee is ground; in fact, the longer you brew the coffee, the more of these compounds will be extracted.

In terms of over-arching tastes, the standard flavor categories apply. The ideal cup of coffee strikes a balance between tastes that are sweet, sour, salty, savory, and bitter; some of the most lauded and complex coffee has definite notes from all five of these categories. Generally speaking, however, the flavor of most concern to coffee drinkers is the sweetness. This is the aspect that is considered by many to separate good coffee from great coffee, as it provides an excellent balance to the coffee's natural bitterness and acidity. You'll find that many of the sweet and sour notes come from the aromatics, while the bitter, salty, and savory notes are from the taste compounds, but this is far from a hard and fast rule.

Acidity

Also described as "brightness" or "sharpness," the acidity of a coffee is different than the sour notes you'll get from the flavor characteristics. Acidity often goes hand in hand with fruit and floral notes, but it is also a texture descriptor, describing the way the coffee feels on your tongue, often on the front edge of the taste. Acidity is one of the most scrutinized characteristics of coffee, in part because a good acidity level is seen as the hallmark of a successful cup of coffee.

If you're having trouble visualizing how acidity is different from a sour flavor, consider the taste sensation of biting into a green apple, or sucking on a lemon wedge. There is a certain physical sensation that accompanies this, a kind of "sparkle" on your tongue, that's different from the flavors the fruit brings.

When talking about the brightness of a coffee, certain descriptors are commonly used. For the degree of acidity, you can use terms like "intense" or "mild." There are also different qualities to the acidity. It can be sharp, edgy, rough, or rounded, or some variation of those, in addition to the varying intensity. It's easiest to evaluate the acidity once the coffee has had a chance to cool slightly, so you may notice it more on your second or third pass. Acidity tends to be enhanced by pressurized brews, like espresso.

Body

You may also hear this referred to as the coffee's "mouthfeel." It can be roughly defined as the weight of the coffee in your mouth. You can also think of it as the coffee's viscosity or thickness, and describes how much presence the coffee seems to have when you're holding it in your mouth. "Body can sometimes be tricky for beginners to identify. If you're having trouble pinpointing descriptors for the coffee's body, try moving it around your mouth for a bit longer before swallowing.

The body of a coffee comes mostly from the insoluble materials that are in it, like the lipids, fats, or fine coffee particulates. These bind together within the cup to form colloids. While these compounds increase the body, they can also muddy the flavor if they're too plentiful within the brew.

Body is one of the characteristics most affected by the brewing method that you use. Different brewing methods will allow different amounts of insoluble material into the cup. Espresso tends to have the most body, both because the coffee to water ratio is relatively high and because the perforated metal of the portafilter allows more dissolved solids through into the brew. Methods that use a paper filter, like Chemex or pour over, will have a lighter body since more of the solids are filtered out. Immersion brewing methods will be somewhere in the middle, one of the reasons why it is a popular method for tastings.

There are many different terms you can use to describe the body of a coffee. If it has a relatively light body, you might use terms like watery, slick, juicy, silky, or tea-like. A medium body will be more like 2% milk—smooth and creamy, sometimes with a syrupy or round characteristic. A heavy body might be described using words like full, velvety, or even chewy. The fuller the body, the more you'll feel it coating the inside of your mouth after you drink.

Finish

The lingering effect of the coffee after you've swallowed it, both in regards to its taste and its texture, is referred to as the finish. You may also hear this called the coffee's aftertaste. This is an important part of the coffee drinking experience. A good coffee should linger for a little while after you've swallowed, though the notes that linger are equally important to determine its overall quality.

The ideal coffee has a sweet, clean finish, with a taste that stays on your tongue for around 10-15 seconds after swallowing. It should reinforce the best notes of the coffee, without feeling too rough or bitter, and should have a similar complexity to the initial taste. There is often a direct correlation between the body and the finish, with a fuller body typically granting a more lingering aftertaste, though there are certainly exceptions to this rule. Similar to the body, the finish will be affected by the brewing method. Espresso tends to have the most aftertaste because of the many oils and trapped gasses contained in both the liquor and the crema.

Chapter 3: Flavor Wheels

The first flavor wheel specifically for coffee was designed by the SCAA in the 1980s. This flavor wheel remained unchanged for over two decades. Its 2016 revision was concurrent with the expansion of the lexicon, a book which established the specific and definable taste that could be associated with each of the 110 contained attributes, giving each one a reference product that is both brand specific and widely available. This revision project was one of the most extensive collaborative research projects ever undertaken for the coffee industry and established a new set of vocabulary for use by professionals and amateurs alike.

The coffee lexicon is a separate document that exists independently of the flavor wheel, though the flavors defined in it form the foundation of the tastes listed on the wheel. It is an invaluable tool for professional cuppers, for the first time giving the industry a standardized language to use when they're discussing coffee notes. It was built by the organization World Coffee Research, in conjunction with a research group based out of Kansas State University, and is an invaluable tool for coffee professionals. For amateur tasters, however, the flavor wheel itself should be plenty comprehensive on its own.

Since the creation of the first SCAA flavor wheel, other companies in the coffee industry have designed their own versions of the model. These are often very similar to the official SCAA version but have variations designed to better-suit the specific coffees utilized by the company. The majority of these were developed well before the 2016 revision that standardized the lexicon; it is yet to be seen how the existence of the new SCAA flavor wheel will affect the use of these alternate versions.

The sections that follow in this chapter will explore in depth two different flavor wheels that you may find particularly useful. The first is the revised SCAA wheel; the second, the wheel designed by Counter Culture, an independent roaster that provides coffee to artesian cafes throughout the United States. If you would like to see a visual representation of these coffee wheels, they're widely available for free online; simply type the name of the coffee wheel you want to see into your chosen search engine. You may find it helpful to print a copy of your preferred wheel and keep it on the table during your tasting for quick and easy reference.

The SCAA flavor wheel

The very center of the SCAA flavor wheel is broken into two halves: tastes and aromas. Each of these is then divided into sub-categories that extend outwards, getting more specific as they go. The "tastes" half of the wheel is where you'll find a lot of descriptors that have to do with the feel and body of the coffee; the "aromas" half is the domain of more familiar flavor names, associated with common foods and ingredients.

The tastes side of the wheel is further divided into four broad sections: sour, sweet, salt, and bitter, the four main established zones of the tongue, though excluding the more recently added "savory" or "umami" region. Each of these is then divided into smaller units which give you an array of potential words that you can use to describe the coffee's taste. Within sour, you'll find terms like acrid, hard, tart, and tangy. Sweet is divided between acidic sweetness (piquant or nippy) and mellow sweetness, with suggested terms of mild or delicate. With salt, the division is between bland and sharp flavors. Finally, the bitter category is divided into harsh terms, like alkaline or caustic, and pungent terms, indicating phenolic or creosol flavors.

The aromas side of the wheel is also sub-divided initially into three sections: enzymatic, sugar browning, and dry distillation. This half is the inverse of the tastes half, in the sense that the descriptors will likely become more familiar to you as you move further out. Within the enzymatic category are flavors that are fruity (citrus or berry-like flavor), flowery (floral and fragrant flavors), and herby (whether alliaceous, like onion and garlic, or leguminous, like peas or cucumbers). The sugar browning section is divided into categories for nut, caramel, or chocolate flavors. Finally, the dry distillation section is where you'll find flavors that are carbony, spicy, or resinous. This last category contains some flavors that might not seem desirable at first blush, like the medicinal category of the resinous section, or the burnt, charred, and tarry descriptors you'll find in the carbony section.

The Counter Culture flavor wheel

There is no central half and half division in the Counter Culture flavor wheel. Instead, it looks much more similar to the tasting wheel that's used by sommeliers to taste wine. It is divided into ten broad sections, each of which represents a different category of flavors which are commonly found in coffee, color-coded to make it easier to navigate.

The most detailed section of the wheel is the "fruit" section. This makes sense, given the prominence of fruit flavors in most coffees. The section is further divided into eight smaller categories, each of which has its own associated specific fruit tastes. These include citrus, apple/pear, melon, grape (which also includes wine), tropical fruit, stone fruit (fruits with pits, like cherry, plum, apricot, and peach), berry, and dried fruit.

The other nine sections of the wheel have only one further layer of division, into specific flavors associated with that group. Working counter-clockwise, the next grouping is "floral." The floral category is comprised mostly of aromatics as opposed to tastes and includes such flavors as hibiscus, lavender, jasmine, orange blossom, and lemongrass. There is often a fine division between these flavors and those included in the next category, labeled "vegetal, earthy, herb." This includes herbs common from most kitchens, like dill, mint, and sage, as well as vegetable flavors sometimes found in coffee, such as peas, green pepper, olive, squash, and leafy greens. This is also where you'll find tastes associated with other growing things. Positive fungal or earthy, soil flavors will be found under this category. If there are notes of cedar, wood, hay, or tobacco, these will be included in this category, as will tastes more commonly associated with other beverages, like hops, bergamot, black tea, green tea, or grassiness.

The "savory" category is relatively small and includes anything that will give you the umami notes associated more often with food. The most commonly encountered entry in this category is a tomato note, especially when it comes to the acidity; you may also taste notes of soy sauce, meatiness, or leather. This is differentiated from the "spice" category that follows to the left, which includes flavors like licorice, nutmeg, ginger, cinnamon, coriander, and pepper.

The next category to the left is where you'll find the notes imparted by the roasting, including subcategories of carbon, smoke, burnt sugar, or toast. After that is a section for grain or cereal notes, things like fresh bread, graham crackers, granola, or pastries, along with raw grains like barley, wheat, and rye.

The three categories along the bottom of the flavor wheel are those that you will likely get the most notes from as you taste, with flavors that tend to be even more prominent than the fruity and floral notes so prized in high-quality coffees. The "nut" and "chocolate" categories are fairly self-explanatory, but you may need to study the entries under "sweet and sugary." Tastes featured here include sugar variants like brown sugar, sugar cane, honey, and molasses, as well as syrupy and sugary flavors in general, like cola, caramel, maple syrup, and marshmallows. Flavors generally associated with baking are also included in this category, with such options as butter, cream, nougat, and vanilla.

The Counter Culture flavor wheel, in general, is designed to be easily used by a taster who's only interested in the actual notes and flavors that hit their tongue and is less concerned with the compound that contributes the flavors, making no distinction between tastes and aromas. It also sticks to flavors that can be considered desirable. This doesn't necessarily mean that every coffee drinker is looking for cedar or smoke notes (for example), but that there are situations in which every note listed on this flavor wheel can come from a well-roasted, well-brewed, high-quality coffee. Counter Culture has a separate flavor wheel for off tastes (explored in more depth in chapter 5), which is different from the SCAA flavor wheel, which incorporates both desirable and undesirable flavors. This can make the Counter Culture wheel a bit more intuitive for non-professionals, helping to differentiate the flavors you want from the ones you don't.

Chapter 4: Using Flavor Wheels

Whichever flavor wheel you choose to use as a reference, the array of options can be a bit overwhelming to someone who hasn't spent a lot of time training their palate. This is especially true of the SCAA flavor wheel, which includes both familiar descriptors and more conceptual terms, like clean, vibrant, and sturdy—words that you may not have a point of reference in your mind for associating with a taste.

The flavor wheel is intended as an aid to tasting, not a detriment. It is not intended to be prescriptive. If you taste something in the coffee that isn't on the wheel, that doesn't mean you're wrong; coffee is constantly evolving, with new varietals, processing methods, and roasting practices bringing new tastes into the mix that may not have been prevalent before. This is further complicated by the fact that everyone's palate is unique. Two people drinking the same cup of coffee might pick out completely different flavors from it.

You also don't necessarily need to use food-based terminology to describe the flavors in the coffee. Smell and taste are two senses very heavily associated with memories and your own background and experiences. You can use words like "summery" or "wild" if the flavors in a given cup seem to align with those terms in your mind. Other non-food descriptors that are common include words like bright, crisp, dull, pointed, balanced, deep, delicate, dirty, juicy, or complex. You can also use modifiers freely, pairing terms like faint, lingering, muted, or strong with other terms to get a more specific and accurate picture of what your tongue is getting out of the coffee. The end goal is to give a purposeful description of the coffee that can communicate its essence in a way that other people can relate to, and a way that you'll be able to interpret and understand when you go back and look at your notes later.

When you're using a flavor wheel, you want to work from the inside out. Start by figuring out which general category the taste will fall into—whether it's floral or fruity, for example, or more nutty or chocolatey. From there, you can start to get more specific, working outward until you've identified the exact flavor. You may not be able to achieve this degree of specificity when you're first tasting. It could be that you can tell there's a fruity element, or even that it's some form of citrus, but won't be able to discern whether it reminds you more of orange or lemon. This is fine, especially for a beginner. Whatever notes you can make, even if they're vague, will help you to better understand the coffee and its flavors.

Also, keep in mind that good coffee won't only have one note. It should be a very complex combination of flavors from various points of the flavor wheel. You may taste the acidity of a lemon along with the sweetness of brown sugar and hints of raspberry or almond all at the same time. Picking these flavors apart from each other can be one of the trickiest aspects of tasting coffee, especially for a lay person. This is why it's often helpful to taste in groups. You may be able to identify the nuttiness, while your friend might have a better perception of the brighter, citrus tones. By working together, you can construct the full profile of the flavor, helping each other to identify the many various notes contained in a given bean.

The flavor of coffee is too complex to really generalize, with too many factors affecting the taste at each step of the bean's lifespan. Having said that, however, one of the best ways for a beginning taster to wrap their minds around the world of tasting is to attach certain notes or flavors with the general profiles of beans from certain geographical areas. These rules are certainly not set in stone, and you'll find a lot of variation between beans from the same region even before accounting for such factors as the roast level or the brewing practices. Constructing a general flavor profile for a certain region's coffee can be helpful, however, letting you get a sense of what to look out for and expect from a given cup—so long as you're prepared for the fact that there will be anomalies and flavors that don't align with what the coffee from a given region is "supposed to" taste like.

Central American regional profiles

Coffees from Central America are often some of the easiest for a beginning taster to work with. They are almost entirely wet processed and grow in a fairly similar climate across countries, which tend to use more standardized growing practices. This combination of factors can give them a more consistent taste profile with fewer surprises or variations.

General terms used to describe Central American coffees include bright, clean, and balanced. They will tend to have a mix of smooth, brown sugar or caramel sweetness with a more tart fruit-like acidity. The texture can be smooth like rich chocolate or more buttery, like a pastry crust, but the body does tend more toward the medium or thin side. Costa Rican coffees are often especially light and refreshing with strong citrus notes, often grapefruit or lemon flavors. Coffees from Guatemala tend to have a more apple or pear-like fruitiness and acidity, while those from Honduras and Nicaragua tend to give you more of a tropical fruit flavor, with notes of mango or pineapple.

You can also include coffees from North America and the Caribbean in the Central American category, as they will often share a similar flavor profile. This includes coffees from Hawaii, which are more American in nature despite the fact that the islands are closer geographically to Southeast Asia. Coffee from Kona is especially known for having an apricot finish. If you're buying a coffee from Jamaica, expect a similar clean taste profile to what you'd get from a Central American coffee, though with a slightly creamier body and more floral than fruity notes.

Coffee from Mexico shows the most variation of any from this category, owing mainly to the differing climate conditions between the regions of the country. Coffee from the Oaxaca region will have the lightest body and acidity, while that from the Chiapas region tends to have strong notes of nut and caramel and a thicker body, more similar to coffees from Guatemala. If there are fruity notes, it tends to be a cherry-like acidity or other flavors from the stone fruit category.

South American regional profiles

While there are certainly many similarities between the coffees grown in Central America and the ones from South America—owing largely to the use of similar varieties, growing practices, and processing methods—but the greater degree of variation in the climate conditions and elevations in turn means there is more variation in the flavor profiles, as well.

Coffees from Colombia tend to be sweeter and less acidic. Though they can be bright with mild fruity notes, you're more likely to taste notes of nut, chocolate, caramel, or maple syrup. You can expect a smooth texture with a medium body from most Colombian varieties. Coffees from the Nariño region will have a slightly higher acidity, owing to the volcanic soil typically used for growing.

The other major coffee-producing nation in South America is Brazil. These beans are grown generally at a low altitude than most others from the region, which results in a cup that's less clean, with a lower acidity and fewer fruit or floral notes. You can expect a relatively heavy body, which may be syrupy or may be creamier, with a lingering aftertaste. If you're looking for flavor notes, expect to find them in the nut and chocolate portion of the flavor wheel, potentially with grain-like or malty undertones.

African regional profiles

Complexity is the main buzz word when it comes to African coffees. If you want to taste a coffee that will give you a wide array of notes from all quadrants of the flavor wheel, African beans are a good way to go. You can find coffees from this region that are processed using both wet and dry methods; each of these will give you a slightly different set of flavor profiles, even within beans grown in the same country (or even on the same farm). This is also the only country that produces wild-grown coffee along with cultivated or farm-grown trees, introducing a degree of wildness and unpredictability into the crops from this continent. Regardless of which country the coffee is from, you can expect African coffees to be fragrant, strong, and full-bodied, with significant fruit and floral notes.

Ethiopian coffees come predominantly from three regions: Harrar, Sidamo, and Yirgacheffe. If they're wet-processed, they will have a thinner, more tea-like texture that's drier on the palate, with a shorter aftertaste. The notes in a wet-processed Ethiopian are more delicate and often from the floral quadrant of the flavor wheel; look for tastes like jasmine, hibiscus, and lemongrass. Dry-processed or natural Ethiopians, on the other hand, tend to be syrupy or juicy in their body and are known for bright fruit flavors. Look for berry notes, like strawberry and blueberry, when you're tasting a natural Ethiopian.

Coffees from Kenya are known for being bold and juicy, both in flavor and mouthfeel. The acidity is prominent but may be more savory than sweet, varying between a tomato-like acidity and a tart, mouth-puckering punch that's more like black currant. The sweetness generally comes from the fruity side of the spectrum. Depending on the region, you may find tropical notes like mango and papaya, citrus notes like orange and grapefruit, or berry notes like raspberry and blueberry.

These are the two main exporters of coffee from Africa, but you can also find beans grown in a whole host of other countries. Coffees from Tanzania are popular in part because the nation's crops produce a lot of peaberries, a genetic mutation of the beans that makes them rounder and denser than typical coffee beans. This gives them a bright, citrus acidity, with a juicy body and floral and fruit notes ranging from jasmine to black currant. Coffees from Rwanda, meanwhile, tend to have an acidity more like green apple, bright and punch, with fresh floral notes. Coffee from Burundi is more similar to Kenyans, clean in flavor with berry notes in both the taste and the aroma and a thick, rich body.

Coffees grown in the Middle East tend to have a similar flavor profile to coffees from Africa and can be considered in the same category for practical purposes. The most prominent growing region of the Middle East is Yemen. You can expect a full-bodied coffee from this region, often with an acidity that's winey rather than fruit-like. There is often a musky, spicy note to the flavor—look for dry fruit notes along with cinnamon, cardamom, tobacco, or chocolate.

Asian regional profiles

There is nearly as much variation between coffees grown in Asian nations as there is with those grown in Africa, and for many of the same reasons: regional variations in growing and processing methods. More so than with any other region, Asian coffees tend to have the assertive, unique flavors that make them a "love or hate" kind of coffee.

This is especially true of the many varieties from Indonesia. In general, these coffees will be dark and earthy, with more savory notes and lower acidity. There are often spicy flavor notes, and the body is typically on the heavier side, especially when the beans have been dry-processed. Because Indonesia is an island of nations, the variations between islands will be as marked as the variations between countries in other regions. Coffees from Java tend to be the mildest of the Indonesian coffees, giving you the cleanest cup, especially when they're wet-processed; look for nutty, malty, and chocolatey notes with a bright acidity and a relatively light body. Conversely, coffees from Sumatra tend to be the most complex and unique. You'll likely taste flavors from the savory and herby portions of the wheel, with a rich earthiness that can be mushroom-like or stout-like. Depending on the variety and the roast, however, you may also taste spicy notes (especially anise and clove) or smoky, roasted flavors, with woody or chocolatey undertones.

Another Pacific island nation known for its coffee production is Papua New Guinea. Most of the coffee crops here grow in volcanic soil, which gives them a bright, clean acidity, pronounced sweetness, and syrupy, full body. You may taste some of the earthiness found in Indonesian coffees, but it more often ends up on the sour, bright side of the wheel, with notes of tart fruits like currant, lemon, and cherry.

You may occasionally also see coffee grown in India. The majority of these beans come from the state of Karnataka, which is often labeled as Mysore (the former name of the state). It is usually wet processed, meaning it has a cleaner cup and thinner body than the coffees of Indonesia, for example, though it still tends to exhibit a similar complexity, combining bright and sweet fruity notes with darker spice and roasted flavors.

There is also a particular processing method, called Monsooning, which is only widely practiced in Asian coffee production. This involves allowing the picked coffee cherries to be exposed to the moist air of the monsoon season for a little while, "aging" the coffee beans and letting them ferment before they're sent through the rest of the process. A monsooned coffee bean will be paler, and the flavor tends to be a milder, creamy, smoother version of the un-monsooned version of the bean. Monsooning increases the body and reduces the acidity;

31

it may also take on a slightly fermented flavor, similar to wine or brandy. This is typically seen most with Indian coffees, though you may also find Indonesian monsooned varieties.

Identifying Off Flavors

Most of the flavors on the flavor wheel aren't inherently good or bad. Some notes are less universally admired than others—especially on the savory and earthy sides of the wheel—but whether they're considered "good" or not is a matter of personal preference. Perhaps more importantly, their presence in the cup is not a symptom of a problem with the bean at some stage of its growth or production. Those are tastes that are naturally occurring, however rare or controversial they may be.

There are other flavors, though, that should be seen as an indication of a deeper ill. Being able to identify a good acidity from the sourness of an improper brew, or telling the difference between a coffee that's moldy and one that simply has earthy notes, is one of the main skills a professional coffee taster has to develop.

The good news for a home taster is that the beans you're buying have most likely already been vetted for quality. You're not deciding which green coffee beans you're going to be purchasing lots of for your roasting purposes; the roaster you're buying from has people who have already seen to that. Still, being able to identify the probable source of off flavors can help you gain a better understanding of the coffee that you drink.

As was mentioned in chapter 3, Counter Culture has a flavor wheel of only off flavors commonly found in coffee beans, conveniently divided by the probable source of the imperfection or issue. You can find a version of this wheel online for free as well if you'd rather have a visual aid for your tasting. It is used just like other coffee wheels, with broader categories in the center of the wheel that branch out to more specific tastes as you go outward. The center-most circle is divided into seven categories: mold, aged or faded, tainted, over-roasted, under-roasted, under-ripe, and fruit decomposition.

A coffee also doesn't have to have any one specific "bad" taste to be a lower-quality coffee. Complexity and balance are two characteristics that many professional coffee tasters look for in their beans. If a bean is said to be flat or to lack character, this is a way of saying the taste experience is too one-note. This single flavor can be a good one, but without other contrasting flavors, it can be one-dimensional, lacking the full taste you want out of your coffee drinking experience.

Just like every step of the process brings out different aspects of potential flavor provided by that specific cultivar or variety, faults and off flavors can come about at various stages of the coffee bean's life, as well. This is important to keep in mind before you rush out to buy that $60 per pound Jamaica Blue Mountain. Just because the cultivar is prized doesn't inherently guarantee its quality; issues with the growing cycle, the processing method, or the roasting can still muck it up. Each of the sections that follow here will explore a step of the process from seed to cup and the potential flavor issues that can arise in each.

Faults from growing

Different cultivars will be at their best at different elevations, rainfall levels, and temperature ranges. The perfect growing conditions for one bean can kill the best potential of another; knowing which beans to plant on which land is one of the first challenges for the coffee farmer.

If a coffee tastes flat or one-dimensional, this can often be the product of faults in the growing process—either a lack of proper nutrients in the soil, a coffee grown at low elevation, or one that didn't receive enough rainfall while it was growing. While coffee trees like heat and humidity, they also don't do well in direct sunlight, preferring the protection of tree canopies in their natural habitat. A coffee that was scorched by too much exposure to the sun can have a flat taste, as well, though it may also have faint carbon or burnt notes, even if it's handled correctly in the roasting and brewing stages. Wide fluctuations in humidity can give the coffee a phenolic flavor, similar to a Band-Aid or burning rubber.

The ripeness of the coffee cherry when it is picked can also have an impact on the flavor. If the cherry was not ripe enough, this could lead to a raw, overly vegetal flavor, similar to a raw peanut or stale grain; you may hear the taste described as "green," which is different than the grassy flavor found in green tea that some find desirable. On the other side of things, if the cherry was allowed to ripen too much on the tree, it can give the coffee a sour flavor, like acetic acid. This may also result in alliaceous notes (like the flavor that comes from garlic or onions).

There are also a variety of pests that like to eat the cherries and leaves of the plants, and these can leave lasting off flavors in the beans. Often the taste will end up being flat and one-dimensional since the beans will be unable to get their proper nutrients as they grow. If the beans have been tainted by the pests, you may find they have a slight turpeny or diesel-like flavor.

Faults from processing

There are multiple stages to the processing of a coffee bean, and multiple accepted methods of completing each stage. Wet-processed beans are removed from their cherries immediately after picking, while dry-processed or natural coffees are allowed to ferment inside the fruits for a designated length of time before being pulped. There are also processes that fall in between these two, called semi-washed or pulped-natural, along with the Monsooned coffee mentioned in the previous chapter. Beyond this comes the question of how the coffee beans are dried after processing. Some are laid out to dry in natural sunlight; others are dried in large mechanical dryers in large batches. Each of the above methods has its own guidelines and correct practices; off flavors often result if these aren't properly followed.

The main off flavors you'll get from problems with the processing will come from the "Fruit Decomposition" section of the Counter Culture off tastes flavor wheel. You can describe these tastes with words like rotten or funky, or by comparing them to tasting like a garbage bin or a compost heap. You may also get a sour note, similar to vinegar or bad wine. Coffees that taste gamey or have notes of animal hide or leather may also have been improperly processed.

Not all of the moisture is removed from a coffee bean during drying. The ideal residual moisture content is between 10% and 12%, depending on the method and the bean. If they're under-dried, this can allow mold to develop within the bean, imparting either phenolic or musty, mildew flavors. If they're over-dried, this most often results in a coffee that tastes flat, losing its complexity, though it can also give the coffee a carbony, scorched taste.

Faults from storage

Once they're processed and dried, green coffee beans can stay fresh for up to a year before they're roasted. They will often sit in a few different warehouses during this time: one at the mill where they were processed, one or more at the importer or distribution centers where they were shipped, and one at the roaster who purchases them. If conditions aren't optimal in any of these places—or during the shipping from one place to the next—you'll taste it in the beans.

Mold growth is perhaps the most common fault picked up during the storage and transportation stage. Depending on the type and severity of the mold growth, this can impart a range of different flavors. It is another potential source of phenolic flavors, although in the case of mold these may be more medicinal or chlorinated than straight burnt rubber. A rotten, iodine-like, decomposing taste is another potential result of mold growth. They may also pick up a musty flavor, a mildewed taste, or a faint taste of raw potato.

Pests can also get into coffee when it's being stored. Both insect and rodent pests are common banes of the coffee warehouse. The off flavors that result from pests at this stage will be similar to the tainted flavors from pests during growing: diesel or turpeny notes, along with a "baggy" flavor or carbony, wood smoke notes.

Even though green coffee lasts a lot longer than roasted coffee, it does still have an expiration date, after which it will begin to go stale. Loss of complexity is one of the most common faults imparted by long storage. The "Aged and faded" section of the off flavor wheel will also come into play; the coffee may take on cardboard or paper notes. It may also have a pronounced woodiness or a taste like stale bread.

Faults from roasting

Over-roasting is a more common issue than under-roasting when it comes to tasting coffee. There are two stages in the roasting process at which the bean splits open to release escaping gasses and steam: the first crack and the second crack. The first crack is an indication that the coffee is roasted enough to brew; coffee removed at this point will be at a light roast level. The second crack happens at the very end of the process, and not all coffees will reach this point. Anything that has roasted to or beyond the second crack will be considered a dark roast.

If coffee is not allowed to reach the first crack before it's removed from the roaster, it will end up having a "green" flavor. This could give it grain-like notes or a vegetal quality, like raw peas. Beans that have reached the second crack (or a temperature of around 450°F) will lose some of their brightness and acidity. These beans are actually preferred by some people, especially as a component of an espresso blend, but won't be ideal for tasting; you'll get mostly roast and dark chocolate flavors. Once a bean passes 500°F, it is officially over-roasted. The flavor notes you'll get from these beans will be almost exclusively from the carbon end of the spectrum, with descriptors like ashy, burnt, or fishy.

Faults from brewing

For tasting, you'll predominantly be using an immersion brew method, so you may not encounter these flavor issues during that process. It's still a good idea to know what problems can arise from the brew, though, especially as you're trying out the coffees you've tasted in other brew methods.

If the coffee was complex during the tasting but flat on another brewing method, it is possible the right amount of hot water was not allowed to make contact with the grounds. A brewing temperature that's too low could result in a sour flavor. An over-extracted brew will often have a chalky or salty feel on the tongue; these could also result from too much water or water that's too hot. A medicinal flavor that gives you a tingling or numbness along the sides of your tongue is also a sign of over-extraction, especially when brewed using the espresso method.

Training Your Palate

It might sound strange to say you need to learn how to taste—after all, eating is one of the only things you've probably been doing your entire life. Being able to identify and name the flavors that are crossing your tongue can be surprisingly tricky, however, especially if you're trying to separate them out from the other bold flavors contained in a cup of coffee.

When you're at the tasting table, your palate will be one of your most useful tools. Learning how to use it correctly can be a time-consuming and tricky process. If the only thing you can think of to say when you taste is that it tastes like coffee, you may need to spend some quality time building up a reference library of tastes, flavors, and sensations that you can use to compare coffee flavors to in the future. Before you can figure out what you're looking for in your perfect cup of coffee, you have to acquire a taste for coffee, in all its subtleties.

Eat mindfully

Studying the flavor wheels mentioned in chapter 3 is one way to build up the right vocabulary to express and describe the tastes you identify in a cup of coffee, but even these helpful aids will be largely meaningless if you don't know what the foods listed on them taste like. Especially when it comes to more subtle differences—say that between a note of lime and a note of lemon—articulating these specific flavors can be tricky if your palate hasn't been trained.

Eating mindfully is simply another way to say that you should pay attention to the tastes and sensations you're experiencing whenever you eat if you're on a mission to train your palate. Pay attention to every aspect of the eating experience, from the initial aroma to the texture and the way it feels on your tongue, along with the more obvious aspects of taste. If you're training your palate specifically for tasting coffee, pay special attention to the ingredients whose flavors are most likely to be part of a coffee's flavor profile—fruits, especially berries and citrus fruits, various varieties of nuts, and baking flavors like cocoa, vanilla, and caramel.

Not everything that can have notes in coffee is something you're probably in the habit of eating by itself. When it comes to things like molasses and maple syrup, picking out those flavors can be tricky if you've never eaten them straight. When it comes to floral notes like jasmine or hibiscus, you can learn them by smell instead of taste. If you detect a certain scent when you walk into a room or walk by a plant, see if you can identify it. You should even pay attention to exactly what makes things taste and smell bad, as well. When you taste or smell something unpleasant, take the time to focus on exactly what you don't like about it; this will be a great benefit in identifying off flavors.

Stay focused

If you're the kind of person who starts every day off with a cup of coffee, you may be so accustomed to the overall profile of the flavor that you can't pick apart the more subtle aspects of the taste. This is the same principle that makes it difficult to detect the odor of the air in your own home unless you've been away for a little while. Being able to effectively taste the notes in coffee means first emptying your mind of these preconceptions, allowing you to get to the true components and roots of the flavor.

Whether you're mindfully tasting another ingredient or sitting down at the tasting table, your first step should always be to empty your mind so that you can focus exclusively on the tastes and sensations on your tongue. Taste is a very fleeting sensation, even more so when you're tasting coffee since the flavor will change as it cools. Make sure you're in the right frame of mind to be able to maintain sharp focus throughout the tasting. This means getting plenty of sleep the night before and drinking plenty of water; your taste buds can react differently when you're dehydrated, and it can also make it more difficult to focus.

Practice makes perfect

Developing a palate that can detect subtle flavors is a skill, and like any skill, it will become more honed with practice. You don't have to be sitting down at an official tasting table to try and pick out notes from your coffee. If you get your beans from a café, they will likely have tasting notes on file that you can look at; if you buy it pre-packaged, these are often on the bag of beans. See how many of these flavor notes you can detect when you're drinking your morning cup—and if you don't get those specific flavors, try to keep track of which flavors you are picking up. Pay attention to the acidity, body, and finish as well as the flavors and aromas.

Remember that taste is a matter of personal preference; there are no right or wrong answers. Whatever you're eating or drinking, pay attention to what tastes you get out of it. To a well-educated palate, telling coffees apart that are from different growing region is as easy as telling the difference between sugar and salt. The more you practice learning the tastes that are in coffee, the larger a collection of descriptors you'll have at your disposal, letting you compare different coffees in a more meaningful way.

Testing your palate

Sometimes it can be difficult to tell just how good your palate is. If you want to test your progress, consider having a friend set up a blind tasting to see if you can distinguish which coffee is which. Have a friend prepare the samples for you without you watching. If you want to truly be tested, ask the friend to buy the coffee, too, so you don't even know what your options are.

The best place to start is to have the samples prepared from coffee at three different roast levels and see if you can determine which one is which by smell and taste alone. Once you can determine a light, medium, and dark roast from each other blind, move on to trying three coffees from different growing regions. Make it easy on yourself at first, and choose one coffee from the Americas, one from Africa, and one from Asia. As you refine your palate, you'll be able to get down to more subtle differences, like determining a Kenya from an Ethiopia, or even between growing regions of the same country.

Professional Cupping

A cupping is the name for the official, controlled tastings that coffee professionals do. These can happen at multiple stages of the coffee life cycle. Owners of a farm will cup the beans from different crops to test them for quality and verify the harvest is yielding the flavors they expect; roasters will cup the coffees when they're deciding which ones to purchase or to combine into blends; and café owners and baristas will cup coffees when they're choosing the right ones to stock on their shelves or use in their drinks.

The idea behind a professional cupping is to remove all possible variables so they can evaluate the coffees on a level playing field. By removing differences in grind, brewing method, and often even in roast level, they're able to evaluate the intrinsic characteristics of the beans, comparing varieties side by side to better make their purchasing decisions. Because of this, professional cuppings will typically have a very stringent protocol in place when it comes to the sequence and timing of events, one that is kept strictly consistent not only within a cupping but across multiple sessions.

There is a fair amount of scientific rigor involved in the process, down to the grading sheets used to evaluate the coffees. The grounds and water are both weighed to a high degree of precision, and the water is often poured using a gooseneck kettle to ensure an even pour. Steps are taken to prevent cross-contamination, not only between different coffees, but between different samples of the same coffee; separate cups and spoons are often used, and the grinder is thoroughly flushed between samples. Professional tasters will also frequently cup blind to avoid having any pre-conceived biases affect their tasting of the coffee.

While a home tasting session can be less rigorously controlled than one done by professionals, understanding the way coffee experts conduct a tasting—and why—will better prepare you to set up one of your own. From the equipment used to how the coffee is sipped, every step of the process is done a certain way for a reason. Though the end goal of most professional cuppings is commercial, the stages involved are all about unlocking the truest flavor of the bean, the same thing you're looking for when you do your own tastings at home.

Setting up

When professionals set up a cupping, they'll often have a station for each sample they're tasting. Each of the samples

47

they will be testing will be weighed out and the whole beans waiting in pre-portioned containers. This allows the coffees to be each ground immediately prior to the brew, rather than wasting time in weighing each sample as you go. This becomes especially important the more coffees you're brewing, to make sure that each sample is being brewed for the proper span of time. Each sample will also have a designated cup into which it is brewed; there may also be a designated spoon for each sample, although there may alternatively be a spoon for each taster, with a glass of water they can use to rinse it between tastings.

Another very important thing that has to be present at any tasting is a spittoon, garbage can, or something else that the coffee can be spit out into. In the same way that sommeliers spit out the wine they're tasting so that they don't get too intoxicated, professional cuppers need to spit out the majority of coffee they drink to avoid becoming over-caffeinated.

Part of the reason professional tasters need to spit out the coffee they taste is the sheer number of coffees they'll be tasting in a session. There can often be slight variations between different beans in the same crop or roasting batch. To account for this—and make sure they're getting a true sense of the coffees that they're drinking—professional cuppers will often do at least three samples of each coffee they're tasting. Depending on how many coffees they're trying out, this could end up being quite a lot to drink in one session.

Brewing

Each sample will use around 12 grams of beans, ground fine immediately prior to brewing. The taster will typically smell the coffee as soon as it comes out of the grinder to get a sense of its aroma. Shaking the grounds will release more of this aroma, letting the taster get a full, hearty whiff. Each sample should be ground separately, with the chute of the grinder cleared completely and the dosing chamber brushed clean between samples to prevent cross-contamination.

Once the coffee is ground, the sample cup should be filled with 5-6 ounces of water just off boiling. The ideal temperature range is the same as other brew methods, between 195°F and 205°F. The water should be poured slowly in concentric circles, ensuring complete saturation of the grounds and looking out for dry clumps on the surface. A gooseneck kettle can be very helpful in controlling the flow of water but is not strictly necessary the way it is for manual brewing methods.

When the water is poured in, some of the grounds will sink to the bottom of the cup, while others will form a crust on the surface. The tasters will examine the crust visually as it's forming, taking note of any changes that occur when the coffee comes into contact with the water. It's also usually a good idea to give the surface a good sniff to get a sense of the aroma and how it's developed.

The coffee should be allowed to brew for around three to four minutes, the same length of time you'd allow for a French press. It may seem strange that such a simple brewing method

49

would be used, with no filter to prevent the grinds from entering the brewed beverage. The reasoning behind this is that it removes any potential influence that more complex brewing methods would have on the coffee. By allowing the water and grinds to maintain direct contact, the full flavor of the bean can be released into the cup. Since the tasters won't be drinking from the cup directly, the grinds that sink to the bottom aren't likely to be stirred up and consumed with the brewed coffee.

This method does mean the surface of the coffee sample will need to be cleaned before the coffee is tasted. To do this, they first take a spoon and break the crust on top by drawing the spoon through the grounds. At this point, the taster should again smell the coffee, taking a deep sniff with his or her nose down close to the surface of the coffee to get the full effect of the aroma, which will be at its peak in this particular moment.

Most of the grounds will settle to the bottom of the cup once the crust is broken. The grounds that stay floating on the surface of the brewed coffee can be scooped off using a spoon and dumped into the spittoon or trash can. This is usually done by taking two designated spoons and placing them at the back of the cup, then bringing them forward around the outer edge in a single, fluid motion. When the spoons meet in the front of the cup, they are scooped up and out, leaving behind as much liquid as possible.

Tasting

Once the surface of the cup has been cleaned, the tasting portion of the cupping is ready to begin. It's a good idea to take a second at this point and forget the aromas that were observed and recorded during the grinding and brewing. The smell of a coffee is directly related to the taste, but each will have its own distinctive nature that a professional taster will try to get a sense of separately.

There is a special technique to tasting like a professional, which is known as "aspirating" the coffee. It is a similar technique to that used by wine tasters to open up the flavor of the wine and reveal all of its complexities on the tongue. A spoonful of coffee is brought up to the taster's lips then sucked violently into their mouth while they take a breath. This technique sprays the coffee over the entire tongue and at the same time draws it into the nasal passages, giving the full array of tastes and aromas. This will make a loud slurping sound if done correctly.

After aspirating, the coffee is moved around on the tongue and through the entire mouth so the taster can get a sense of the mouthfeel as well as the body. Sweetness and acidity are the main points of focus. The taster should note the ways the flavor changes and develops the longer it's in their mouth— whether it gets stronger or flatter, sweeter or softer. Once this step is completed, the coffee is either swallowed or spit out and the aftertaste noted.

This procedure is then repeated with each sample on the table. Every coffee around the table is sampled once, then the taster goes back to taste each coffee again, noting how the flavor has changed as the coffee cools. It is important to note the flavor at various stages of the brew; some characteristics will be easier to discern at a cooler temperature, while others will only come through in the initial taste.

Evaluation

Most professional tasters prefer to stay relatively quiet during the cupping itself. This is both to avoid distractions, maintaining their focus on the flavors themselves, and to prevent having their tastes influenced by the opinions of others at the tasting table. The mind is very susceptible to suggestion; hearing what someone else tasted in a coffee could sway how the other tasters feel about it, as well.

Once everyone has had a chance to get their first impressions of all the coffees, there will often be a sharing of notes and opinions between all the tasters. These results are then written down, with notes taken about the coffee's aroma and flavor, as well as its sweetness, acidity, body, and finish.

In a professional context, many tasters will give the coffee a numerical grade or score once the cupping has concluded. This is traditionally on a scale of 1-100 and corresponds roughly to school grades (90-100 equals an A, 80-89 equals a B, and so on). A numerical score doesn't necessarily need to be given to understand the coffee, however, and many professionals object to this kind of rating system because it reduces the complex combination of flavors in the coffee to a number that ignores the subtleties of the beverage. Regardless of how the evaluation is recorded, however, some kind of record of the tasting experience is key, in both professional and home tasting contexts.

Home Tasting Practices

A home tasting does not need to necessarily follow the same stringent protocols as a professional cupping. Some aspects of a professional cupping—like the grading form filled out at the end, for example—are more confusing than helpful, and often end up being detrimental to the home tasting experience. You should enjoy the coffee tasting, first and foremost. This process is about honing your own skills and finding your perfect cup, not adhering to the standards of a given roaster or coffee shop. Whatever tweaks you have to make to the professional cupping format so it better suits your lifestyle are perfectly acceptable.

Certain aspects of the process do benefit even casual tasters to employ, such as the unique way the coffee samples are brewed. An immersion brewing method is generally the best for bringing out the full flavor potential of the bean because nothing is filtered out. If you'd rather not go through the skimming process described in the previous chapter, a French press will be the best alternative, though it will mean sacrificing the formation and breaking of the crust.

In the same vein, it is a good idea to taste the coffees you make during this process without adding any milk or sugar, even if you would add them to the coffee you drink normally. Anything you add to the coffee is going to change its flavor, obscuring the complex and subtle notes the bean has to offer.

Preplanning

You can do your tastings either alone or in a group. A group setting is often especially beneficial for a beginner because it gives you some people to bounce your ideas off of. Where professional tasters don't often communicate while they're tasting to avoid bias, if you're still training your palate having other people around to tell you what they taste can help you articulate your own discoveries. Keep your mind open to other possibilities, but also don't be afraid to tell people what you taste, even if it's different than what your tasting partners say.

If you are tasting in a group, make sure there are enough samples for everyone; you'll need to make at least two samples of each coffee for a group of four or more. This makes sure everyone isn't trying to crowd their spoon into the same cup, and that everyone gets the experience of cleaning a cup and smelling the aroma released after you break the crust on top.

Once you know how many people you're going to be tasting with, you can buy the right amount of coffee for the session. If you're buying coffees from a variety of countries or regions, try to get coffees that are close to the same roast level. It can also be enjoyable to taste various roast levels of the same region of coffee, if that's an option that's available to you. You can always roast your own green beans at home if you can't find different roast levels of the same coffee in the store. Sampling coffees from the same country but sold by different roasters or coffee shops can also be an interesting experiment, though you will be looking for more subtle variations between them than if you sample coffees with more variety.

Setting up

The first thing you need to figure out is where you're going to do your tasting. Remember that you'll need to have a separate container for each sample of coffee that you make, along with containers to hold the whole beans before you grind them. If there are multiple people participating, make sure they have enough room to move around without bumping into each other. A kitchen is often the ideal location, especially since it also gives you quick access to other tools you'll need, like your kettle and your grinder. Lay out your supplies before you even start weighing out your beans; it'll save you time and stress in the long run.

Organization is important. When you're preparing your samples, label or color-code them so you can tell which is which if they get moved around on the table. Proper organization also means staying consistent with your timing and preparation. All the coffee should ideally be ground to the same degree, use the same coffee to water ratio, be brewed at the same temperature, and have the same brewing time. If there are inconsistencies in your process, you could end up tasting those instead of the differences in the beans.

On the day of the tasting, you want to try and preserve your taste buds as much as possible. Don't eat or drink anything with a particularly strong flavor during the hours before the tasting starts; this holds true during the tasting, as well. If you want to provide snacks, do so after the tasting is over. If you're a smoker, do your best not to smoke immediately before (or during) the tasting, as this can dull both your smell and taste.

The tasting

Look for the characteristics that have been discussed in the previous chapters—not only the notes and tastes, but also the acidity and body. Evaluate how clean the cup is and how much it lingers on your tongue. The taste and length of the aftertaste can be excellent indications of the quality of both the beans and the brew. Feel the weight of the coffee on your tongue and compare its textures to other things you've had to drink. Is it thin like water or tea, or is it creamier, like milk? Whatever you taste, write it down in your tasting journal. Have notebooks or sheets of paper for the other members of the group to do the same.

It can be easy to wear out your palate during a coffee tasting. The flavors in coffee are so strong that they can easily overwhelm your taste buds if you drink too many in a row. Flushing your mouth out with water between coffees can help. You can also keep unsalted soda crackers at the table to nibble on between samples as a palate cleanser.

Whatever variations you make to the tasting process, remember that consistency is the golden rule. Do the same thing with each sample, and preferably the same thing every time you taste. As you continue to perfect your technique and hone your palate, you'll be able to pick out ever more subtle notes of the coffee, expanding the value of the tasting in your life.

The Full Picture

It can be argued that coffee tasting is even more important for finding quality versions of the beverage than it is for wine. When you buy a bottle of wine, it will be labeled with a wealth of information—the type of grape, the year it was bottled, and the region it grew it. Finding exceptional wines can sometimes be more about memorizing the ideal characteristics outlined by other than it is about finding those high-quality offerings yourself.

A bag of coffee will not give you such a comprehensive picture of the contents. It will be labeled with the country of origin, and typically the roast level; if you're lucky, you may also get the name of the region or the cultivar. Not only is this not enough information to truly give you a picture of the coffee's flavor, there is more variation in coffee than there is in wine. Changes to the climate during the harvest season can completely alter the character of the bean; changes in the processing, storage, and roasting can be equally impactful.

Coffee professionals have to be more active in their selection process than sommeliers. New cultivars are frequently being produced or tried in locations where they haven't been grown before. As the world's climate continues to shift, areas that were once prized for their excellent beans have become less consistent, and vice versa. When it comes to the world of coffee, there is always something new to be discovered.

Deep understanding of coffee flavors is often best achieved through comparison. By lining up several coffees side by side, you'll be able to note the differences and similarities better than you could by tasting a single coffee in a vacuum. The more coffees you taste, the more points of comparison you'll have for the next, and the better you'll be able to pick out the beverage's distinctive notes. Learning the terminology will help to speak more knowledgeably about the things you're tasting, but there is really no shortcut to developing a strong palate. Doing so requires a lot of time and practice. The good news is that practice can be both fun and rewarding, opening you up to the full range of flavors that high-quality coffee has to offer.

Win a free

kindle
OASIS

Let us know what you thought of this book to enter the sweepstake at:

http://booksfor.review/tasting

Want to

supercharge

your coffee knowledge?

Turn this page...

Also available by

Jessica Simms

Blending Coffee

Your Guide to Coffee Blends and the Perfect Cup

JESSICA SIMMS

I know coffee

Harvesting,
Blending,
Roasting,
Brewing,
Grinding,
& Tasting
Coffee

JESSICA SIMMS

Harvesting Coffee

e Life of a Coffee Bean from Planting to Processing

JESSICA SIMMS

Roasting Coffee

How to Roast Green Coffee Beans like a Pro!

JESSICA SIMMS

Brewing & Grinding Coffee

How to Make Good Coffee at Home

JESSICA SIMMS

The
I know coffee
series

Steaming Milk

Want that Perfect Latte or Cappuccino?

JESSICA SIMMS

Making Crema

The Art and Science of the Perfect Espresso Shot

JESSICA SIMMS

Printed by Amazon Italia Logistica S.r.l.
Torrazza Piemonte (TO), Italy

10790999R00041